BUILD YOUR PERSONAL
BRAND WITH THE UNIVERSE

AUTHENTIC YOU ACHIEVEMENT

**FOCUS ON THE JOURNEY, LOCATE THE
DESTINATION, AND CHAMPION YOU**

NELSON

Vue d'asile

AUTHENTIC YOU ACHIEVEMENT

The information in this book is based on the author's knowledge, experience, and opinions. The ideas and methods described in this book are not intended to be a definitive set of instructions. You may discover other methods and materials to accomplish the same end result. Your results may differ.

Published by Vue d'Asile, Missouri City, Texas

Printed in the United States of America
First Paperback Edition - November 2025

Paperback ISBN: 9798218825577

Edited by: Khloe's Thoughts Editing
Khloesthoughtsediting.com

Cover and Layout by: Make Your Mark Publishing Solutions
www.moniquemensah.com

"Life's greatest enemy is not time, it is you."

In memory of my primary spiritual mentor
in eternal medication, FATHER.

"Life for all in its anguish is ours…"

~Ferdinand Lyle, *Penny Dreadful*

A successful you requires falling in love
many times, always with the next you

QUOD SUMUS HOC ERITIS
(you will be what you are)

THE ARCHITECT

The Architect is not just a man; he is a presence; a force that exists quietly yet profoundly in one's life. He does not impose himself, nor does he demand recognition for the weight he carries or the lives he changes. And yet, his influence is undeniably subtle, life-altering, and deeply woven into the fabric of who you are becoming.

There is something about the way he listens as if he is not just hearing your words but mapping out the unspoken layers of your thoughts and fears. He sees through the masks you wear, not with judgment but with an understanding so profound it feels like he has already walked your path. His ability to interpret what has been and what is yet to come borders on the prophetic. It is not magic—it is wisdom, born of battles he has fought and scars he has earned. To know his mind is to stand in the presence of something extraordinary, something sacred.

He is the male figure one longs for in the darkest moments of childhood—the guide one never knows is needed. But he is also so much more. He is a best friend who does not flinch when confronted with the rawest parts of your soul, a mentor who offers you the tools to rise from your ashes without ever taking the credit for your ascent. Like the mythical Tree of Life, he nourishes those around him, even as he silently wrestles with his own struggles—his own storms. He is rooted, grounded, immovable—a symbol of endurance and growth.

What makes the Architect awe-inspiring is his ability to create space for one to rebuild yourself. He does not hand you answers wrapped neatly in absolutes. Instead, he gives you the tools, the seeds of possibility, and lets one choose how to cultivate them. He does not need to say much to change everything. A single sentence from him can strike like lightning, illuminating truths one has avoided or could not see before. And even in his silence, there is a kind of reassurance—his presence alone tells you, "I believe in you, even when you don't believe in yourself."

What humbles one the most about the Architect is that he is not invincible. He has his own battles, his own moments of doubt and pain. Yet, he carries them with grace, never letting them overshadow the support he gives to others. He does not use his struggles as an excuse to step back; instead, he uses them as a reason to step forward. Watching him navigate his own challenges with quiet resilience is like witnessing a phoenix in its own cycle of burning rebirth. He shows you that strength is not about never falling—it is about how you rise.

His mind is a gift—a labyrinth of wisdom, insight, and perspective. To know it, even in part, is an honor. He has the rare ability to see not just who you are but who you could be. And somehow, he holds both versions of you—the broken and the potential—with equal care. He does not push you to move faster than you are ready, but he never lets you settle for less than what you are more than capable of.

The Architect is not simply a pillar of knowledge—he is the embodiment of elevating your mind. He does not just teach you how to survive; he teaches you how to live. He does not just help you see the light at the beginning of the tunnel—he shows you how to build the fire by assisting yourself to light your own way. His impact is not fleeting or superficial—it is the kind of change that rewires your very being, leaving one forever altered.

To have the Architect in your life is to know that, even in one's most destroyed moments, there is someone who sees your worth yet even more understands your value. Someone who will remind you, with words or silence, that you are not definable by your pains but by how you choose to rise into and then from. And for that, you are not just grateful—you are forevermore challenged amongst change!

Written by: LWC

"The anvil of justice is planted firm, and fate who makes the sword does the forging in advance."

~ Aechylus ~

"In essence you are the creator of your own fate(s)... forged from the fire of your own creation..."

~ Nelson ~

OPENING

I n reading, you shall identify that only you can find the exact coordinates to offer grace to your you. In my view it takes an overabundance of different works compiled, to assist completion in obtaining the baseline body of you in constant progress. I am merely suggesting that the greatest thing at a point for clarified saneness is to separate for you to become learned about the fault line in you! If not, when the next known point arises, you could continue giving something away that you do not understand but can feel deeply within understood. This not knowing your viable unknowns, is how fragments continue getting loss or discarded about on a trail of misguided tears. I implore your understanding to conceptualize that you are the infinity of time. Believe in the self-sustaining arc reactor that is YOU…

YOU-preneurship – the in-depth personal pursuit of devoutly plunging into self-accountability, undertaking all calculated responsibility in discovering your authentic value. Prioritizing the organization of your life's development as methodically as a business, in promoting you as an advanced brand to the universe.

The first time I got lost, of this now I am going to discover myself...

~ Nelson ~

CONTENTS

THE AXIS THAT IS YOU...

Did you know once released; a baited breath's weight is measurable through lung volumes? The air we exhale is heavier than the air our system filters during inhale. Perhaps spawning the term, "get rid of dead weight." This is a writer's embellishment of course, the term; not breath accountably calculations. When you comprehend this, you will know your YOU. Perhaps even be at the tail end of the beginning in acceptance of YOU! Are you your own dead weight in portions? The importance of not cheaply giving your space away is invaluable. It is going to take placing yourself on the rat trap several times to mature your rotation. You will come to understand your distinctly unique pheromones density. Pain is something that beckons, a call answered far too often, and you need to befriend YOU. There is a song that Bill Withers sang called *Friend of Mine*. The line from that song, "might be that we have different views sometimes but that's alright, you're still a friend of mine." True and not; the not is not knowing willingly when recoil must be applied implementation during situational circumstance. Investigate to know that solitude is an invaluable spiritual gift. Just ask and look to the universe for your answers! Once you embrace this as more than just a notion, you will realize the conscience of said and not simply the slave mentality worth of you... The time has come to stop running and now walk to the core of value in YOU!

Loving yourself to death shall never compete with loving you to life... Come with...

PHILOSOPHY

REFLECTION

SELF-ABUSE

The routine of abusing yourself is the equivalent of internal Stockholm syndrome. Abruptly obliterate that defiling prowess from your sanctuary. This habitual ritualistic redundancy is an unaliving "La Petite mort" as referred to by the French that will be exhausting. It is not enough to experience exhaustions during the find of YOU, which is the actualization of the discovery of all lifetimes. This awakening of sorts if you believe in reincarnation, shall propel your atoms rebirth quantum forward. Why? Because you exist as the true multiverse. Take me for instance, I have no siblings, yay me! However, this means I possess the innate ability to be the only, middle, and eldest and I have. For what did I learn during these interhuman phases? I did a great deal of self-retrospection during that crawl, with the universal key in view and now cradling it in my hands with additional time on my life sentence. YOU and YOU alone will never achieve control. Command of you is the better biggest championship. Wonder why I did not say win or winner? Well, we are all winners in some capacity, everyone can win a game, but can you champion your specific cause through the journey? Life is not a game nor should be referred to as such. Now the winner vs. a champion. The paths in your journeys are comprised of several wins plus losses. The greatness of you has it in you to morph beyond the simplistic qualities of a winner, the Champion significances the totality of the quest. You must champion the cause of YOU! Again, solitude be a friend not foe and time shares both introvert and extrovert climaxes garnering wisdom. For even the fool possesses tendencies of the wise. You do know when to say enough am I finished with this, it is when speech ceases to articulate. Come to trust the silent internal you more than the process that binds an act. You want to be boundless, more positive and less negative stored kinetic energy for YOU.

It is time, time to end what was and being what is, breathe as only the most authentic you for the first time.

4
PHILOSOPHY

REFLECTION

TRAUMA PARENTAL

Was it or is it still the best of times perchance the most dreadful or a whimsical capricious mix there of? The following words shall not linger. The shadow existent visibly hidden demons that grayscale haunt you must be expelled henceforth immediately over time. Identify with this statement as the need for an exorcism of them from you, in whatever way deemed sequential. Believe me, you can exonerate the presents of your future. What indubitable mis-rendered educations have your parentals bestowed plus stored involuntarily voluntarily? Perhaps the futile counsel of unpreparedness and disorganization that one day you can take control of your life through inadequate preparation beguiled in this futuristic embryonic world. Good, bad, and indifferent to whatever it is, the time has arrived to induce the crematoria effect. Memorize that nothing really works if void self-answerability, referred to as karma. Toro Nagashi is the Japanese practice of floating lanterns down rivers or into the sea to honor and remember loved ones who have passed. Your spirits require guidance to where they belong in the eternal after. I embrace the ceremony as the light amongst the darkness an inevitable ash cleansing by water. An understanding of the conductive field while immersed in water to the spiritual realm, research to enhance your knowledge. You can and should, when the need arises honor the old you and at the same time detach from what ails YOU. The incorporation of becoming well versed in a plethora of tactical measurements is vital. You should assist in helping yourself hypothesize accelerants that prolifically combust into the extraordinary YOU.

Do not make all of what you know about you, imagine the more in plus around you...

4

PHILOSOPHY

REFLECTION

_____
_____
_____
_____
_____
_____
_____
_____
_____
_____
_____
_____
_____
_____
_____
_____
_____
_____
_____
_____
_____
_____
_____

REJECTION RISK

How are you with handling rejection? You must risk rejection to be successful in funding you. Far too often, the weight of acceptance is unfortunately placed on the love of and like from others. Upon this quest you must grapple then grasp, that you have spent a small fortune of life rejecting your you. Consider that most of us will forgo our own true directness of words, confidence, likes, adventure, business, personal dreams, beauty, and the greatest love(s) in fear for other's contemporary company. Is that genuine love of self? Please, I ask. It is not selfishness to be selfish in getting to you. I asked a mentee once a decisive question within turmoil. Are you willing to sacrifice your happiest for your wife's or family's happiest. When one is single, sacrifices must be performed in the stance of youth, which encompasses the early twenties. Not saying both are not achievable, a line exists in the understanding of acceleration whether with family or single. Forge today as the end-being of real genuineness with self-first, YOU! Start with making the love of you the greatest option. Remember, it is better to select from options than to be dwindled down forcibly to a choice. On your spectrum of understanding, you should be the choice and not look at yourself as an option. When the family union exists lean to communicating your needs, do not just abandon your present. For those who are single, capitalize on the vantage point as the course.

Promise yourself nothing, "be of your word" to you...

REFLECTION

THE HEART

C an you transform the pressure of your inanimate wants into adamant needs? The human heart is not a mystery yet the most sought-after of treasure, cease toying with what yearns to be understood in you. For the heart wants what it wants when it wants it, but is it what it needs. The heart is a muscle that must be worked out regularly irregular in initial developments of self-trustworthiness. Living for your love of you will complete the following: Love of self sharpens, too firmly shaping the love within you. In possible decades, your heart has existed in fragments already broken desiring a reprieve, again love you. Abuse of the forebears holds court in your guarded kingdom of chaotic peace. You have also attributed to the mounds of disorder. Never only take what you can get once more, the moment has arrived "TAKE WHAT BELONGS TO YOU!" The road less traveled is really traversed by many. Lie with no person, place, or thing that will stain your entrails to petrification. Bring forth the conspiring artist and paint or construct your masterpieces. Mature in the understanding of the duality of meaning in words. Abstinence, it must morph into spiritual ritual boundlessly. Recognition of unrequited pain must venture beyond simplistic foresight.

Why? Because we request foresight as a natured afterthought reactive response to displeasure. Proactiveness is what we are seeking to boost. See your heart as the life thread of business, that only you hold the straps of soul ties to. Feed your heart what is needed for success, maybe you know in clarity that you have only been surviving thus far. Strength of heart is the primary sender block of your internal pyramid. Talk to your heart daily of your mind. C.T Fletcher, talks to his muscles during workouts. He believes you must get into the mind of your muscle; it is an all magnificently magnifying quote, "Grow expletive GROW!" The point is to not complicate the growth of YOU. A path in sovereign solidarity awaits YOU. Love you and only you until you understand how to love you and then contemplate colliding into another's spirit, knowledgeable peace filled.

Become your own peace, then perhaps be the harmony adjoined with a partner...

4
PHILOSOPHY

REFLECTION

BECOMING

Becoming you requires ultimate self-sacrifices beyond measurement. Initially, you will need to achieve unfounded spiritual, mental, and physical disciplines. This discipline is the isolated solitude of a monk that takes the vow of silence. All impurities must be flushed through individual chambers then the waste purged from every pore. Your you must sit amongst the asylums of past postpartum, seeking the freshest rare present that evolve upon luminous futures. Explore destinations looking for YOU. The only obstacles that have possession of you are within the portion of you that can only be removed by you. Be more than willing to own your expansion. Numerous considerations must be taken, but your internal development of brain waves must instill a white noise system; paramount to establishing the truth of YOU! What is no longer for you must be withdrawn immediately! The longing to run instead of crawling shall beam as the light from Heaven, not the blue sky. Blue skies represent the ceiling. Hesitation will cause your you further detriment and potential retreats in concession. So, how do you get into self-isolation is the question? Cold turkey is the best guide and starting somewhere is foundational. Stop adding questions to the till as you have been taught and pick anything or everything if you are at wits beginning. Remember, shite days are soon to be encapsulated in the distant. Being tired is not enough, exhaustion still not justified to remove stagnation, and not until you fill yourself at death's door several times that is when. When you continue to speak on finding you, you are still lost looking. Words do not and shall never supersede raw refined actions. It is going to take evolutions to realize you are not the one that should not be unhappy, at the expense of all others. It may take even longer to recognize; the statement includes family, especially the top tiers. To move in silence, you must mold the mind as such repeatedly. Different primes yield reassessment at interchanging seasons. Remove the word "hope;" it is the misguiding flaw, allow the belief in self to ooze from all pores. When thoughts become claustrophobically petrified that is when the first breath in you awakens. Nothing of old has a chance, a six-figure salary will no longer spark a flame. Walk right to the edge of perceived insanity and leap to the freedom in YOU!

Motivation – Research Les Brown, what practice makes you.

The interpretation for me was the first person that should be forgiven, is YOU!

REFLECTION

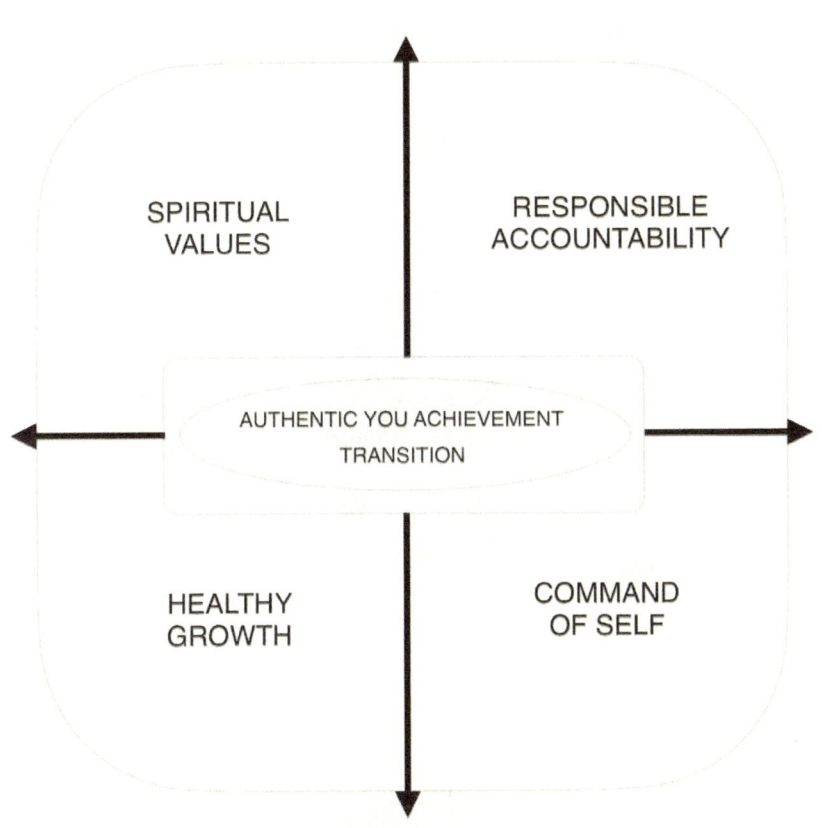

SPIRITUAL
VALUES

RESPONSIBLE
ACCOUNTABILITY

AUTHENTIC YOU ACHIEVEMENT
TRANSITION

HEALTHY
GROWTH

COMMAND
OF SELF

AYA - AUTHENTIC YOU ACHIEVEMENT
Phase 1 TRANSITION

CONNECT WITH AUTHENTIC NELSON

SCAN ME!

FREE GIFT INSIDE

DISCIPLINES INSTILLED IS THE HIGHEST FORM IN BECOMING YOU

Is life solely about self-preservation or more than surviving? Merely stating what else is there in a world built to destroy belief in being human by humans. Do you know and even better believe in you? To be clear, a level of commanded selfishness must be obtained then strummed in your core anticlockwise. What are your standards of self-care? Have you located that it factor, venturing into your own space to captivation. After the mouth full, what say you about you? I remember Jada Pinkett-Smith saying what she wants is "to learn how to love." This has nothing to do with being a fan, rather the arduous truths within her caldron's honest rant! Do you know how to discipline yourself beyond what you are taught? This world is a swing state propaganda persecution farming system. Cliché as it sounds, red or blue pill of self-disciplining. Which do you consume? Clearly it would be the blue pill at this point, Neo! Do you crave the need to own who you are? The answer is sacrifice through DISCIPLINE! Even within my written pre-programming, a code exists to free myself, that one word is the foundation <u>DISCIPLINES</u>. Can you deprogram you from this worldly conundrum? There is a sheer difference in connection to the world and connection with the universe. The individual seeking to be one with self within the galaxies gravitational pull of thought establishes disciplinary procedures. Seeing with heart, continuedly growing mentally understanding with mind, and viewing no color through irises. Stop this game of hide and seek from yourself! You are the matter that matters, the grandest find known to humankind. Life is too often acquainted with the game of chess; I submit that life is complex for most not complicated. The comparison is to the level of commitment in achieving grandmaster status. Of this present world you must come to lose the absolute taste for just about everything then rebuild through discipline. You are a league of disciplined internal shadows.

From out of your darknesses, allow the first light to perforate edges and remain lit.

PHILOSOPHY

REFLECTION

SEPARATIONAL SACRIFICE

For your embetterment will you separate from hive mentally? The initial time for me was a demonstrative proverbial beast of forced persuasion the discombobulation was mind breaking. A decade plus I did isolate once again though self-induced departure. Dropped everything without a pulse just for me and should have never gone back. The detail of hindsight is not worth mentioning. Magnifying is this self-imposed detention. I became the ample healthiest version of self in four months through handpicked sustenance at my eldest year. My renovated stream was of brilliance. In furthering the conversation of separating yourself, it is the way. If that part of life is still on your side, enhance the properties of YOU. Meaning your worldly ties breathe minimal. Living a minimalist lifestyle is a reward filled with serenity. The mystery of what the daily entailed. Mornings began with a four a.m. meditation—sea moss, homemade elderberry syrup, tons of Mountain Valley throughout, stretching, and a two-mile run that I often pushed to four. Arriving onsite working still fasting from 6:30 p.m. from the previous day until eleven-thirty a.m. The system began to only live for greens that I cut and a fresh beet juice blended concoction. Lunchtime was a quick drive to the gym for two more miles on the treadmill. The snacks were nuts, berries, peanut butter, and raisins. ZERO processed sugars, alcohol, or consumption of flesh. My room had no television, and the only vice was an occasional cigar. I became narrow, which in turn morphed the mind broad.

Leave when you must, you can always return or not...

4
PHILOSOPHY

REFLECTION

SUSTENANCE

A word containing supreme visions in aspirations of healthiness. What concepts do you have on nurturing behaviors? This nutrient rich hydrating elixir sustenance, as the messenger offered Earth and Water to Leonidas. Possesses entrapping qualities about the senses in belief that you are consuming glory but could instead be dining on cannibalistic demise. What is the point of the statement, both items were once conceptionally free for a short extension before pollutants. You must green fuel you as earth and profusely hydrate your reservoirs. However, sustenance might contain falsehoods of deception in the stance. View this intake as the processed food industry. Handpick items concisely for your garden. You are an individual garden of life. Presentation is not everything, few people have the fortitude to decline gluttony when faced with something engagingly opulent. Everything that glitters is not platinum. Develop an elitist clean consumption view at every moment when it comes to you. Not facially but be a snob when it comes to the protection of you.

Learn to live nutrient enriched...

REFLECTION

LOVING YOU

Do you genuinely love you? If you cannot say yes with a high percentage in confidence, that you love you well the horizon is steadily adrift. Can you openly love someone else that is not you, when incapable of loving self? Love in its flavorful essences be the greatest of interests that evolve immense pleasures to the soul's palette. Understand this revelation through dry and actual tears plus inaudible screams. You should show ultimate pursuits in acquiring perception of what heightens the senses and increases the pleasures within. Not being happy, knowing the foundations of what that word even means or understanding yourself, but being with someone on the pretense of love, breeds chaos. This chaos represents the smoldering internal you seeking next level oneness with self. That you, a tsunami tantrum in a relationship. A bull catching breath in the China shop upset at its now fractured reflection. Discipline through celibacy represents the highest path to seeking the stable physical love of you. Meditation offers divine mental awareness to loving you. The culmination into both commingles into the trinity guiding you spiritually to loving you. None of which paths are easy once the fruits of each have been repetitively improperly sampled spoils. I subscribe to the third eye, being the heart. Your heart yearns for the peace in you.

Love – *L*ive *O*pen to *V*enturing too the *E*xpansion of YOU…

REFLECTION

_____

_____

_____

_____

_____

_____

_____

_____

_____

_____

_____

_____

_____

_____

_____

_____

_____

_____

_____

_____

_____

_____

_____

NEGATIVITY

Does not playing devil's advocate make you akin to the devil in some instances? Assess how negative you are to you? Best described by the words, out with daily decay and in with fresh self-awareness. Break about from what the old guard infused as helping you. Seek assistance, you can help yourself! Dispel word phrases like do not forget, hope, and saying things like "I don't know" when clearly you do! Instead of "don't forget," tell yourself, *REMEMBER!* Forgo the word "hope," it is the gloom to potential downfall and can possess one to forever be practice driven. As I was once, the selfish confined space collector of my words. With the phrase, "I don't know," you station yourself within self-doubt. Be concise in your decision process for you. No other individual can understand you better than you! Not even your mother! I explained to my young adults that at some point you must help yourself and I will only be assisting you from time to time eventually. I take issue with referring to adults as children. It is my opinion that it stifles growth in the now world. What is better helping someone or assistance? When you consistently help, you become the enabler of situations. By assisting another, you establish boundaries amongst your collectives. You do not need help at some point, you require assistance. No one does it alone so do not be lonely! Learn when to share yourself, that is especially with you.

Forge the balance between negative and positive properties within you.

PHILOSOPHY

REFLECTION

SHARING

How can you be against you? Are you constantly taking advantage of yourself? What does it mean? Do you give to too much of you away to undeserving external influences? Such a conundrum, the time trial is analogous to weaponized sharing self to victimization of you. _The 4 w's_; Why, When, with Whom then to What dimensional bandwidth. Give seconds to taking responsibility for your actions. When to pull back and reassess within self-awareness. Caution or being cautious can be a detrimental steeplechase. Be aware of you in all values! When my now young adults started driving, I would always say be aware of your surroundings as well as the people that surround you! I became conscious of just how particular phraseology can and will influx upon an infantile mindset. Infantile does not refer to diapers, but more so like teething. Take for instance the use of "you know better" vs "be better to you," it assists in molding the muscles of the mind constructively. Remember, the journey at core genius is to seek your you. Soul Ties: it is the emotional burden part of the definition, not the spiritual connection yet both may require detachment or even implosion. The term "implosion" in psychology, also referred to as "flooding" allows a patient to expose themselves to their own worst fears. This practice suggests a person that confronts those fears can work through them to diminish that power over them successfully. A deceit goal would be to figure out how to reduce indecisive lag time of nonsense. When mostly younger, we allow lengthy abuse from others unaware of the consequences. In the years to come, carryover blanches you when vehemently you understood time had expired on a person, place, or thing. Work on a system of dropping weight that drowns you void water. Would you consume expired milk? That should invoke your mouth to tighten at the sides slightly cringing. Now liken that experience to allowing another an appeal continuously and you now imprisoned. The flesh is momentary, the spirit is everlasting. Always take accountability for what you have done and or are doing to you. Balancing happiness is only achievable from recognition through finding self to the coherent knowing and then constant refinement. It is only at that time of believing in you and after that your most sacred constellation should share you.

Resist the wanting need in sharing yourself to the lacking quality as another's indentured servant...

PHILOSOPHY

REFLECTION

CONTINUED EDUCATION

Just how much do you comprehend, specifically retention of information during segments of learning and how you access the library? It is not adequate to want additional luxuries and needing more security is a fleeting thought when at struggle. The mandate is you must walk the enlightening maze no matter the scripted darkness looming in the direction of your successes. All triumph is not schoolroom degreed; the world is the largest collegiate training facility. Want is a tantrum and needs are infantile pressures that rarely materialize when thoughts keep a common impeding nature about themselves. A risk reward mentality requires advance developmental sacrifice; you for you! The privileged have sponsors that provide the steps and polished pampered steering during rendering, but more than likely you are not that fortunate. People think just because you have watched something, you should be able to replicate the grandiosity. Recognize that visual learning and applied knowledge are different entities. Sustained monitory progression is a secretive order, and educational evolution often habitually ivy league concealed. All human processors are not crafted correspondingly, and manufacturing is different from pure creation systemically. Providing context, creation is a small batch happening regardless of the sum's sheer expansion vs Ford's assembly line or assimilation is a craft. To venture beyond the word communal, better run to the parallels of discomfort pacing yourself close at center. The world incubates plenty of others that have attained that which you crave. So, educate yourself through countless hours of self-advancement sessions. Keys given thoroughly throughout reading, YouTube, seminars, research, ear hustling from another table, free classes until you can purchase, bonus disciplining yourself to isolation tunnel visions warrants dedication. Be so entranced in the development of you, that the workday or whatever attempting to pull you from your zone has null probability because your transcendence be impenetrable. What is your will, willing to gross?

The system of education is not a failure, once you realize that experiences and you are your greatest teacher...

PHILOSOPHY

REFLECTION

MENTOR(S)

How have you been mentored in your past? Do you have a mentor presently? How will you signify them in the future? While it is possible to have two or more mentors at a time, there is something said about the quality of one voice connected to the universe at individual intervals initially. It is that one voice that grounds your soul spiritually to a defined purposeful understanding about your life's mission. Remember, the mission(s) will change as you level up with age and more position. Why are mentors regularly viewed as immaculate voices only, that you should listen to for proper motivation and pats on the back? Telling the truth though, seeing more so and hearing is learning mentally that you must grow to know how to separate, disseminate plus decipher. Simplified high frequency levels do not balance without low level situations before jumping to another plane of presence. I vetted a friend for employment once through a not-so-great company. Straight to the point, the individual wanted to quit. I explained that this would end the mentoring process effective immediately. When you refuse to teach you how to manage self in the tough, the greatest moments are almost worthless to your till. Fast forwarding, the guidance obtained during those time trials can balance the scales of view.

Now, that individual would not turn away from that experience because of the benefits they bring to the present table when measuring events. Now evaluate your past and question unbalanced mentoring you were forced to receive. After the pains, I once failed to understand the significance through perceived lessor mentorships. I now understand to love me more through all the advice of them all equally. However, now I search when needed the rolodex ravenous upon the knowledge aching for a prior mentor's word I have converted into self-wisdom. I get this all the time, "I need a word from you," and often I barely have words for myself because of the universal commitment established. That is when every syllable is accounted for, during insanity. The clinical definition of the word of course, the repetitiveness of expecting a different outcome on the spot, from the mentee as a mentor. Mentors are the nutrition once finally driven from the comforts of a nest and versa if you have never had that traditional footing. The exchange of that union is not a dictatorship of sorts, it is the giving offering. You will eventually fare even greater when you have a sponsor. A sponsor is a person who sees the door of opportunity, walks you to the door, opens the door, looks at the table of people making decisions, points to you, and says, "Y'all need to give the person a chance and I'm gonna stay here until you do it," Dr. Alifee Breland-Noble.

Recognize the strength in a chance meeting of a few mentoring words of an acquaintance but seek productive sponsorship...

REFLECTION

FALLING

Tired of falling yet? Falling will certainly not leave you! Often it is the right of passage from chapter to chapter. To mention one chapter or chapters can complete a season. What you are working to accomplish is the reduction of types, how hard, and number of falls. Perfection is merely just perception, and I am a Virgo. The sign that is said to live for flawlessness. One is only that at death the aforementioned. If I still thrived for perfection, what would, or could I honestly accomplish? A reference to command verses control directly. Be kinder to you! It is perfectly fine to be hard on yourself, but there is a line! A stumble to fall allows stagnate movement to adjust to the ever-moving target. That stumble is just practice at the days end to the next beginning. Tell yourself you are alright, but do not forego what is required to heal from a fall! Carrying that baggage to the future changes your acceleration point.

Never fear the fall, falling is a gift to standing in advancement…

4

PHILOSOPHY

REFLECTION

SHUT UP, LISTEN!

Ponder in this thought, do you talk too much? Stop sharing so much with everyone else about your strategic edification procurement! Differentiate, are you building revelation for everyone? In my case yes, but here is the dispute. Is distribution on the broadest scale with outsiders while conversing still questionably suitable? For definite full-on particulars are absurd in consciousness. Have a couple of confidants in the circle of trust that genuinely cheerlead your present aspirations to future materialization. Dissemination of entire plans are to be issued in proper increments; believe in the four levels of friendship and research theories of friendships, which are to be considered business relations. Do not under any circumstance repeatedly reach out to people that refuse to offer similar identical solace. Salary exceptions can be discussed to progress; however, your actual earnings certainly not! I guarantee you are encouraging others to demand your coins as their backup piggybank! So, what are you listening for exactly? For your heart to not only speak, yet unparalleled communications. Intake the sereneness in the rhythmic pleasures within your chest cavity your unique metronome thrives liberation. Now *"quiet your mind"* and start living your frequencies. It is equal to a medically checked pulse pulsating. Recognize that multiple conservations must become first in availability of hearing your direct infinite guidance from the universe. Steadily leaking pertinent information is not a successful corporate trait and you are the establishment. Think in terms of blocking a blessing, not blocked deferment, and to forever prolong overlooking this allowance does not productively breathe. When one does not hear, then they fail to listen and how much time is being repetitively wasted? Certain voices must be insistently muzzled, *money talks, wealth whispers*! Longevity exists on the motion of whispers, the wind does not tell you it is coming, it arrives in an abrupt whistle. Where does the philosophy derive from? The centurion intellect of my one-hundred-thirteen-year-old direct descendent. Words did not move him to action; his actions sparked preservation. The system has coerced us to think that suppression of sound is horrible, but for years I released nothing to develop a stable mental voice, for myself. When feeling too chatty, retreat and share only with your shadow. You can only tell on yourself!

Not "just do it, <u>do it now</u>" through imaginable aestheticism movement perhaps in Renaissance…

4

PHILOSOPHY

REFLECTION

BEAUTY

People want the latter portion of a Cinderella story without the growth of pains. Think about the adaptation of the story into the Cinderella Man. The beauty of you is yours to discover, lose, and rediscover then amplify! Understand that if you elect to not work within societal norms, inspect the path you have chosen. The world does not have to accept your beauty! I even question if it wants you verses the universe. It the world will however drain and source the beauty within you like evaporation to your last droplet. What do you allow to affect the thought process on your beauty? Values offer your code the credence of patience. Can you work the long position? Again, never refer to your life as the game, demolish negativity, glance upon no other with disdain, and love your own individual beauty above all. You can be sporting just not hunted or hounded as sport. Beauty is what you are, and everyone should not taste of you from just a feasting of eyes. It is not what you see, rather what your heart builds through feeling. Make how you live your beauty your special thing, and people will adhere to your rotations. What matters is what you think and feel about you, not the world about you. Yes, acceptance is a huge thing, and it may take time to acquire your people or circle. Just understand that we are out here wanting to meet you!

The world, much less a person, cannot tell you what beauty is, being beautiful belongs iconically to you...

PHILOSOPHY

REFLECTION

THE PATH

Reminder, the specific path is yours and yours alone to meander; however, this does not refer to being lonely. Are you afraid to walk it out? Well, be aware, not afraid! Denial often stunts growth in the direction of stagnant personal productivity. Quantum leaps in locating you are sought-after late-night cravings. In essence, the pathways to your compass of righteousness yearn you. A book to further educate is "you2", a similar quick read shedding enlightenment onto the beyond portals of progression. Translation of the old process was step by step, diving into rewiring your harness of considerations allowing divine structure to acceleration. This brick road is pathed with intent filled gems. A few of them lead to it is never too late to stop or move suddenly when requiring somewhat more than that now. Of course, the need changes as you thrive. Like a vampire's carnal thirst, you can only deny the calling for so long before the final call. The paths are immortal. You on the other hand are not. They will await your next arrival. Transform within the season when the path in you realizes change.

Start reminding yourself that, "nothing plus no one will deter me from my PATH!"

REFLECTION

ACKNOWLEDGE YOU

You must understand the depth in value of acknowledgement in further developing a grander you! Acknowledge you and your thoughts before giving something to anyone else's cause due to the potential side effects. What are your standards, needs, wants, and do you want to do what has to be asked and answered? Is it something that they themselves can complete? You are not the doormat for another's to-do-list! What has gotten you hung up destitute even? Get to your reflection and say I LOVE YOU and I am in love with me! Then ask yourself just how much do you need to love yourself? Clearly an unquantified digit. The love you give to you should be as infinite as time and space, reach further than the most distance plant Neptune and wider than the Pacific Ocean expanse, which is sixty-three million miles. One of the best daily affirmations, "I Love you," thought until you can think it louder, then you speak it daily and next complete both more than too often. Internal evolution is not a mystery to be withheld. The exploit is the upstream swim of Alaskan salmon. Live in the awareness of you today, that is what is meant by promising tomorrow or the promise of tomorrow. You are setting expectations of daily task completion and now prepped for whatever is coming. In fact, every day is promised to you, acknowledge dealing with the physical time in hand anything beyond is unrequited pressure focusing on the now forget tomorrow. Be of your present what you do not like to be called, words you don't like to use or in your presence, how you don't care to be handled, and what type of service you prefer when about the town. Develop a formula to how people will acknowledge you by your daily actions. Make it your life's mission to acknowledge your purest of basic needs and you!

Acknowledge yourself as the *MVI*—most valuable individual—to be loved by you!

PHILOSOPHY

REFLECTION

TRAVEL

Operating how the world wants you to, is a salary existence. The work of progression in how the universe beckons you to be is You-preneurship! Remember, all words were and are created and the abundance of you is the ultimate procreation. Ample abundances stream from the tuned perception that you generate and regenerate from the lowest vantage point to your reward. Everyone can operate from the Golden Eagle view in wingspan. Prioritize your commitment to levels of joy, stability, earnings, playing hard, working efficiently, and so forth formulate multiple disciplines. You are at the helm of your ship, make no excuses for the courses and how you steer about in life. Reinvent as many times as you must and answer to your own unselfish needs above the selfishness of others. What kind of traveler are you? Have predetermined limitations or accouterments of your mind back held you? Are you doing what you love? Paul McCartney of The Beatles acted in a Fidelity commercial in 2005. "This is Paul. He's been a coordinator, Beatle, wingman, poet, father, frontman, producer, business mogul, painter, and if that weren't enough a Knight." Never allow the amount of labor required to stop you from being the traveler!

The universe is looking for your uncharted footprints across the world!

REFLECTION

DREAMS

Do you dream in black and white perhaps in the brightness of color, portrait even, maybe panoramic? The way you dream directly imposes a subconscious juncture in how you live. Black and white caught in the matrix, in color you not only stop to smell the flowers but you are the novice botanist. Portrait one-two dimensional given the position of subject matter and panoramic the traveler in the dream. I prefer the brilliance of zoning to conscious daydreaming window shopping. So, what is the significance of dreaming and the side effects? Dreams and stressing can develop the brains correlation patterns, strengthening problem solving, and they advance perspectives. All of these are crucial in becoming rounded and life's creative progressive approach in adaptiveness or lack thereof absence. They also store important gaps of the past and future endeavors. It is the space where the spiritual realm speaks clearly. When I was still running from reality, I fell asleep submerged neck high in the conduit water. I had taken only showers for months attempting to avoid this precognition process. From beyond my fathers, mother grabbed whole of my mental. She simply reached out to me to soothe the chaos and had been awaiting the moment. As much as dreams grant, they similarly extract power, just ask the potential or kinetic energy discombobulated insomniac. Note that the soundest of sleep is immeasurably colossal in the proficiency of you. Choose not to sleep with fear.

Bury all your horrors one by one, the stillness of relaxing bed slumber summons you...

REFLECTION

TECHNICAL ADVANCEMENTS

Technology is the stale breast of death from which we painstakingly suckle. The ulterior motive is to divide you from realism. It is the physically touchless vermin, a terminal infestation of the masses to click past occupying an actual life, the current luminous black plague and true pandemic. Did you see that coming? Technology "the *Culture*" of societal enslavement. Captured by an infant's crying in a restaurant recently, at peripheral glance the booth elevated from his highchair. I thought it was that, but noticed in his fluctuations he would stop when the phone was in hand. Essential assessment, what is the necessity in your use of the network? Most spend 1,700 hours at a monitor, the equivalent of two months distributed over twelve. Delivery drivers have handhelds, we GPS to the gas station, online purchasing is a farm, and phones are a nonessential nightlight. I concluded that I was not intelligent enough to wear a smart watch. There is only so much deliberate Pink Floyd "comfortably numb" activity you need, your brain is the initial high-tech. Establish immediate balance in the areas of virtual verses real space for history repeats itself through perceived innovation. Provide this personal space disruption with the enjoyment of living your tangible life.

Stop making the misstep of technology until bedtime, disconnection is irrefutable by nature...

REFLECTION

IRRITATING QUALITIES

One of the most irritating qualities for me is a person who tiptoes into your space, says nothing, and awaits you to address their need instead of speaking. Then there is the progression halter, those are types that watch your movements while stopping their own and then will manage your direction as though you are incapable! It is a form of control manipulation. What are your irritating qualities? Have you been tiptoeing the same ways against your you? One can forever recognize disdain for others. We are visually taught this at the outer surface realm, learn to blue block that part of you. The idea is to reduce stress, unwarranted strain, mental damage, and affected sleep. It is a good trait being able to love one for who and how they are, but minimum dosage is best. More importantly, identification of your own faults is an invaluable quality of possession. The authenticity in eradication of self-irritations must be a constant revolving door tasked asset. Irritants are discomforts that forge interchange stationery. An attainable goal would be to understand that all qualities can offer you insight into self-improvement.

The inadequacies of irritation of self must be minimized…

REFLECTION

HEAL

D o you truly believe that healing you is a more than possible property? For fact, the process is initialized through healing vocabulary, visual agreement, journaling to reflect upon just what you need to expunge plus extras. I am not a fan of the right or wrong terminology, what's done is done. You will no longer attempt to right the wrong within somebody else forcibly! What are you going to do about you? Remember you can run but not hide long enough from fears, so crawl your way face forward out! Closure must come in a variety of ways. What ways are you willing and able to accept? Often, people desire face-to-face verbal exchanges, but honestly the people that harmed you are probably still lying in the same puddle suffocating. Why would you dare revisit that lack of an experience one last time? Set yourself forward by reaching beyond the discomforting faction now. After forgiving self and oppressors, remember to never forget that all toxic parties are certainly not to be allowed reentry to your Kingdom of Enlightenment. Furthermore, the peace that you maintain becoming is a maturation that many shall never aspire to achieve. Claim your healing by moving differently, in your heart of hearts place stringent demands on healing. Without question the time is yours to take, just ask yourself how much is too much?

Your seeds of healing must be planted upon arrival of each season, remember the necessity of proper hydration...

PHILOSOPHY

REFLECTION

COMMITMENT

Of all the commitments you have or will make, why have you not completely committed to repetitively sustaining growth in you? Move to transcend you! Think about the countless and note worthless endeavors you have taken up. The two-hour sleepovers from one to three a.m. on your phone aimless. Most of us are afraid of the word, not when it comes to other people, but with ourselves. Do you not love or even want to understand the magnitude of your value in volumes? We are an encyclopedia, a living breathing doculife. You are the beauty of a book, housing infinite additions fiending fulfillment. How about commitment to understanding and proper placement of your outgrowing! Dedicate your life to specific goals that offer a level of guaranteed commitment to the universe. The union provides spontaneous expressions conjoined in unification. Obligate yourself to monetary stabilization, sustained health, continuous working out, and caring spiritually. Stand ceremoniously upon this very moment, building a foundation that you shall construct from the wreckage of what once was and shall never again be.

Balance your commitment to you through graduated assessments at none and established life intervals.

PHILOSOPHY

REFLECTION

COMMAND

Control is a whim of hope never to fully materialize. How has your futile efforts in doing such worked out thus far? Your control over something is limiting like a timestamp; however, command of you is the sought-after prize. In my mentoring process these two words are foundational to the understanding of you! Your development over the years is altered personally by hallucinating in being in total control. Leaders COMMAND then demand the highest degree of excellence. To achieve this charm of brilliance, you must look deeply at your movements within you. Is your world out of control but you still want to direct others? Is your house in order, your own personal regimens defined, how do you move spiritually about, and do you window shop or people watch in care or malice? Are you the hand of old trying to transition from inquiring about meaningless information? Translation do you ask questions of people you clearly know the answer to, just to disrupt the fabric that flows because of your shortcomings in waiting to control the situational scenarios.

Self-command is about asking yourself questions and supplying an educated meaningful answer in strengthening you.

PHILOSOPHY

REFLECTION

OVERTHOUGHT

Live misunderstood for who you truly are, change who you are for you, embrace the genuine you to suit yourself or embrace your genuine self to suit you. Others do not really count when it comes to translating your scripts. Breathing most comfortably in your skin is the life you need to live. Never overthink things when it is about your wellbeing! You can tell when you are overthinking, anxiety and shortness of breath happens at the same time. Who likes a sweaty palm? Do not avoid this instinct by going along with others pre-programming. You need to work to the center of the clam amongst chaos and your thoughts. Perform toward always being present of your thoughts to calculation and allow the outer world to overthink on your actions. Why should you be confused or befuddled? Again, it is the reflection of your gut feelings when your gut churns, that is your you activating.

Overthinking happens not when you do not know, it is when you now better understand you!

PHILOSOPHY

REFLECTION

MENTAL HEALTH

W hy is the world suddenly enamored with mental health? The world is no longer just about the mental health of the power-driven male along with just one type of person controlling the health system. Are you wasting away too much or the lack there of mentally deficient? Your mind will be the hardest prison to escape. When you think of escaping, you are setting yourself up to potentially return to another type of destruction. What comes after the navigation of escaping? What you are seeking is complete solacement and must be studious in varying degrees of proactiveness. People that embrace causing any level of mental harm can be removed, your mind must implement the kill off switch. Be coherent that you were never introduced to stabilizing your mental capacity beyond western medicals, medicines, and methods. Simple coping mechanisms are like being taught to just pass a test. How do you feel when someone is managing you? You have to treat you as a human, which is something missing from most of everyday life. Before you see the sex or situation, view the individual as the human being and learn to love yourself as such. Above all, when you need help get the help you need and then assist you in being more to you first!

Unconditional love does not mean unconditional tolerance; this unlearning is vital to your mental health!

REFLECTION

NUTRITION

How much death are you consuming? What you are eating is killing you and you understand this in silence yet again. The history channel and the foods that built America is the base commitment to ruling you. Consumption is not just food! What you ingest will kill you before you die. It is the source of chronic controls. Flower and water make papier mâché paste, our body's internal infrastructure is not equipped as the originals. We do not sweat as they did to release toxicants hourly forging the bond with diabetes as an example. They did not but could have gorged themselves if they wanted the ancients. Present day, food is alien; a foreign substance of betrayal. Allow the math to math for a moment. Nothing with a two-year shelf life and more that is not grandmother canned yields a factor of nutrition. Falsified foods are chemically altering your behavior and modifying your quality of life. It is a weapon identical to modern medicines. The additional mind cluttering experience is having to read a label of ingredients that are unpronounceable! Understand what you eat and eating less I have found is actually better for you. Believe it or not, fasting is the procedure of nutrition that allows the body to process what you have eaten properly.

Swallow what you must until you can taste what you enjoy.

PHILOSOPHY

REFLECTION

MEDITATION SPIRITUALLY

How often do you connect with your higher power? You are the source of your own motives and motivations? Recharging and charging through the solitude of medication rewards one's soul within illumination. Think of the need to grow into the connection with being in love with you. You must plant and federalize yourself. Be spiritual in the thought that the darkness does not only represent burials. The everything began as darkness and seeds are planted in darkest of soil. Yoga is an active meditational vibe that represents poses fostering internal spiritual inconclusiveness. Conceive that even sleep requires some training in this now. The mind must be allowed to actively soften, a skill regularly undervalued. Noise must be void of the experience, you need to learn how to anchor yourself and begin to listen to just your breathing patterns. It's hard to give yourself over to ease to receive space and time. In yoga, I experienced the pose referred to as Supporting Child. It is about supporting the body's needs, and for me connected a puzzle piece from childhood. Embrace the understanding that you are more than capable of all things. The pose requires a yoga bolster, like an oversized pillow. Meditation is not about just what you know, it is about the release of worldly control of you unto the spiritual universe. This space is the essential comfort in tuning your trinity. Hydration is not just water as you become fluid.

Dedicate you to a mediative discipline and never give up mastery of your mind, body, and spirit.

REFLECTION

SELF-ESTEEM

Exuding self-esteem is extremely paramount to define you! Do you have it and to what measurement? Does your esteem have a steady daily presence? I held a study once on confidence vises being direct. The findings concluded that a person using what they not only knew but understood in direct conversation exponentially boosted their self-esteem. Look at it as putting the cart before the horse. Simple word-play changes redirected their focus to speaking to the base knowledge they understood and that made them visibly confident. That directness made them research the answers and call with solutions for the occurrence with just prior low-level knowledge. Esteem within self should be the sole belief in relying on the firmest trust in you. If you do not understand your own valued abilities, warrant self-respect from yourself and are not assertive in dissemination with you, what principles do you stand amongst? I find it hard for one to believe in their own breath without formulated disciplined principles. You can stand for something and still fall. The question is, is the tool teachable? The answer is yes when you are willing and learnable.

Your present surroundings offer more than you receive, work on your development of soft and hard skills to deploy stronger self-esteem.

REFLECTION

WORKOUT

The proven greatest single cure to stress resolution and mental clarity is working out! Develop positive reinforcement for this process improvement and that will be your body thanking you. Working out is a pay it forward system. Stop wishing for the body you cannot have and after reading this chapter start working toward the achievable goal. Working out is the state of mind yet another thing to add in never having sound direction when not an athlete. A general route to understanding your needs would be breathing patterns, foot mobility, stretching, walking, and moving your own body weight. Watch the people around you move. The pain that walks about the facial expression of their body. Never be afraid of getting old, be aware of being sick as you level up in age. Working out reduces the aging process drastically. Stop working out just in the spring for a summer body or a fake new year's resolution. Also, working out is more than just being in a gym. Working out should be the partner to food if not more. Breathing ten cleansing breaths three times daily and as needed is a prize. The use of your feet should be to ground your body to the earth, research specific exercises that only take minutes. Stretching must be actively completed so that you can continue to jump out of the bed. Walking ten thousand steps is also proven and two miles should be dedicated to a treadmill or nature walks to heal more naturally. Weather conditions should never be a deterrent and people definitely not. Changing you should reduce your circle; however, your network determines your net worth.

Alchemize your physical prowess by self-transforming more than your physique.

PHILOSOPHY

REFLECTION

CAPITALIZE

Capitalize not take advantage of you. Taking advantage almost implies misusage to the disadvantage point. Remember, word play is crucial in improving. You want to manifest the chance to benefit from you in recognition of your value. You should have monetary value in mind but out price the market humbly. Capital gains are about what you are afforded once the knowledge is ascertained plus sustained, not what you can afford. I no longer want to walk as a commoner. Meaning to be able to move without risk of contrary consequences. The detriment of never finding you for most is a miner note on a mass level. Unfortunately, as time fades, we begin to yearn for more than what we have simply been given. Taste mature and if you do take the chance to provide you with personal internal capital, what are you doing? Remember, do not take advantage of yourself, rather capitalize on your future. It is exceptionally acceptable to fail faster to succeed in beginning your original aspiration. Pay yourself in results, extra time cannot compare to being result driven. Instead of working on yourself, dedicate every moment asleep and awake to you.

The eye on the prize is to maximize the stake in you.

4

PHILOSOPHY

REFLECTION

REGRETS

would like to say regret nothing you have done; however, we all understand that is near unachievable. We all feel noteworthy repentance and disappointment over past happenings. How about you make amends for the most recent receipts still in your possession! This is like the ninth of the twelve-steps program of AA. Written in 1938 and published in 1939, this is an example for me that some parts of you do and do not need to be changed or completely removed, just tweaked a little. I am sure several things are just too far gone and do not merit groveling in regurgitation. That level of sought-after detailed distressed apology can be mentally sickening, and you can lose yourself again. How about fixing you and maintaining a positive new circulating atmospheric pressure about you? What can be done are tiny foundations established in honor of some of those missteps through guiding others, of course that is once you understand you. Removal of those triggers would be a healthy accord. Drive to an agreement within and resolve all conflict inside you.

View regrets as fallen flower petals, fertilizing minerals of foresight nutrients for forethought.

REFLECTION

HISTORY

Be genuine in the forthwith look that you take histori-
cally to achieve the authentic you. Sugarcoat nothing
while assessing what you have done to yourself! The physical attachment of us or the spiritual assistance impact that I
offer in our going relationship. I asked someone once, "what
is more prevalent?" Swiftly, the reply was the spiritual guidance of your universe connection. Then why do we both not
yield to spiritual interaction solely? An even more balanced
question, why do I not only offer us what is best being of
the knowledge. When you offer or leave someone better you
are being authentic. Have you been leaving yourself better?
You are the doculife. Your past cannot control the present
plus your future needs to have its turn to breathe unabashed.
One can manipulate honesty to a faction of an opinion. Your
history says it all among the black light. How do you treat
you and what do you lay down for repeatedly bludgeoned?
I explain to more males than females now, that it is the old
scent that you still refuse to let go of attracting the same type
of energy. That statement can be applied to the type of jobs
we look for, areas we stay in, and never really changing lanes.
We are a mere microcosm of reinforced historical negligence.

Debunk that negligence and your onion's core will reveal itself. Embrace the great cry that your history is a story not to be rewritten but an exposing trilogy of evolutions.

An individual's particular history does not have to consecutively repeat itself; you have the power to swim to change you! Self-assessment means self-assistance equals the goal...

PHILOSOPHY

REFLECTION

COMPROMISE

Learning to compromise is another thing that got you into not knowing you. You must take this space back through consistently earning your own trust back. Just how often do you second question yourself? When a compromise is met you have sacrificed a portion of you. Learn how to walk within the length of the journey this time. It is not a one-dimensional marathon yet an eventful XTERRA requiring disciplines a multiplex of endurances. Is giving you up a valuable compromise? Just resolve and not fix what you need in you from their atrocity towards you and yourself. Often that means you must remove something over and over until you can no longer compromise yourself. You either agree or disagree and stand on your position unless knowledge of the why is matured to agree. The phrase never compromise yourself is based on two parties that once disagreed. Compromise is as simple as hitting the alarm to snooze.

Stop compromising what you need for wants, reposition your structure to evolve beyond having to befell you.

REFLECTION

CONSISTENT

Consistency is about piecing together what is needed at the active moment. When deployment of skills are most resourcefully in dependency of you. So how consistent are you? In being the greatest you can be, ambition must be huge on paper and of high-def quality visually. The reasoning behind this understanding is that once you wrap your hands amongst greatness the achievement will become minuscule. Your system will become Sahara Desert thirst driven to the grandeur of madness. You will be the two fallen mice in the barrel of crème. It is not enough to be simply motivated because that could happen to process good or bad actions. You must have moral values in consistent successions of you. Embrace championing your own true direct confidence to consistency with you.

You must morph consistently in preparing to pass the torch each time to an evolving you!

PHILOSOPHY

REFLECTION

DESIGNING

Designed thinking comprises five unique stages: empathize, define, ideate, prototype, and test. Ask yourself these five questions. Who do I need to be in life moving forward? How do I need to feel daily? What do I need to offer along this journey now? What do I need to receive from the world? How do I plan on communicating seamlessly with the universe? In the process of designing a concise you, understanding your brand cannot be left to chance on any scale. You are the architect and engineer constructing the infinitely tuned instrumentation. In performing the action of you from cocoon to metamorphosis nothing can be taken lightly for granted! Come to understand what sways your sensibilities, the aesthetics that please you, run several time trials, refine the interlining of the shell, and then release your manufactured goods.

Build yourself into a human of superior mental development, articulating powerful speech, and upright in stance…

REFLECTION

PROTECTION

Protection of your peace should be the only thing about which you are always mindful! Give thought to the number of times you protected people that have done less for you and will continue if allowed. Do you really understand what protecting someone is? Do you inclusively protect you? Blood may be thicker than water, but if you ask most people who hurt them on the planet, family is more than likely the culprit. The secrets that are affecting you must be released! Was it a mother or father that loved your sibling more? A stepparent you were left with and was neglected? Perhaps your own deflection of ownership of a situation. When you do not protect you, you are failing your system's initial structure.

Your house must always champion the complete awareness of protecting you...

REFLECTION

MORALS

Where do you stand, and have you established your set of morals? We think we have set morals based on what we have been taught. More than likely, you do have a foundational set of morals but remember the world changes with every rotation! What was once a measurable moral code almost no longer existing, but you must turn your heart's compass on! Look around at the level of gluttony of all things immoral plus consider the mass number of people willing to sell themselves. I am not talking about judgement of what others elect to do, rather what you do. What is your goodness or badness meter? During a tough conversation I was once asked, "What does your heart say?" So, I am not referring to the simple right is right and wrong is wrong theory. Morals are based on your feelings of treating you with a higher code and then others. It is the rumbling that appears in your gut of decision-making. One of the only times your subconscious is clear of your conscious. Never rest on your morals. Yet another thing you must afford first to yourself by you! Believing is the moral standards of your Heart of Hearts.

Morally stand by overseeing yourself through kindness...

REFLECTION

THE COLLECTIVE IN YOU

The slope is extremely slippery when it comes to your mental collectives. My kids and I, when they were little, used to say, "your cheese done slid clean off your cracker!" Unbeknownst to my seeds, it was my way of masking insurmountable pains that needed more time to become surmountable. How many of your *you's* can you recognize within your collectives of internal thought? You are not crazy because inside different *you's* speak up at contrasting times and talking among the collectives is more than acceptable. The drunk person will speak their truth. Why be drunken for pains to activate the voices? Have the encouraging moment to find the way you need to experience life. Live to think in a conciseness of clarity. Hard yes, but impossible no. It is very pertinent to be of a concise decided speaking voice. Depending on your present position, remember life is about achieving the grandest and grandeur of you.

Recognize than respect the collective of personalities within in you…

REFLECTION

THE UNIVERSE AND YOU

The universe will continue calling, are you prepared to listen now? I implore you to please hear the final call and answer. You are physics bound matter and energy, atoms awaiting a fluidity of limitless connection. A body weighing 154 pounds contains approximately seven times ten to the power of twenty-seven atoms. Your DNA houses a swarm of electrons accompanying protons and neutrons surrounded by electromagnetic properties. You are a complete nucleus, that you in solidarity own. Become the accountable atom to this universe that you desire and that beckons you. A universe, which you are, is crafted to purge, and everyone will eventually receive atonement comeuppance when time is due. Be concerned with working on the rotation of you. Regardless of your past, be initiative-taking in your present and in the future. You will blossom achieving the unabridged YOU!

Knowing you is within itself, knowing the Creator…

4

PHILOSOPHY

REFLECTION

THE BEING...

S o, how did I? To complete the last loose chapters the old world held one claw or talon in me until I sent this to my editor. My old pains developed new ones, and I had to pay homage for 72 hours of neck, back, numbness that rotated throughout, filleted a middle section of an index finger, losing and finding the ear cushion to my Airpod Max and my basic spelling broke down. I blocked out every distraction and voice within my command while the outside world continued its attempted manipulations. In a working progression of combat consistency, cold turkey was the way. Through forceful mental discipline at every manageable moment in weakness until I assimilated with the universal understand of self-completion. The reinforcement of finding my you, was not supposed to be easy, yet it morphed sublime. Formulating the habitual ritual of doing what must be done, right then at the now incision. I forged myself to never neglect my thoughts, feelings, and to not function as though I was balancing. I proved to myself through presentation my newly acquired natural intent. Always offering the internal genuineness, it matters not the type of individual(s) I converse among conversations were always real; however, they now speak in the next level authentic revelation conclusion. Competition or competing with my inner self to conform no longer exists, the word was replaced with confirmation complementing myself and others as we are in separate acknowledged growth stages. I gave the gift of patience with others and especially to myself. The universe taught me that we are all companions pathed differently heading to the same destination and respecting another's placement should be a regal event. No one arrives simultaneously coherent to the knowing of our you! The circle of pure thoughts are larger than life itself to be embraced by the understanding of others' position and regardless of said, at the forefront must be loving you first always.

PHILOSOPHY

REFLECTION

"A LETTER TO MY READERS. "

Loving yourself to death shall never compete with loving you to life. Come with… It is time, time to end what was and being what is, breathe as only the most authentic you for the first time. Do not make all of what you know about you, imagine the more in plus around you. Promise yourself nothing, "be of your word" to you. Become your own peace, then be the harmony adjoined with a partner. The first person that should be forgiven is YOU! From out of your darknesses, allow first light to perforate edges and remain lit. Leave when you must, you can always return or not. Learn to live nutrient enriched. Love – Live Open to Venturing to the Expansion of YOU. Forge the balance between negative and positive properties within you. Resist the wanting need in sharing yourself to the lacking quality as another's indentured servant. The system of education is not a failure once you realize that experiences and you are your greatest teachers. Recognize the strength in a chance meeting of a few mentoring words of an acquaintance but seek productive sponsorship. Never fear the fall, falling is a gift to standing in advancement. Not "just do it, do it now" through imaginable aestheticism movement perhaps in Renaissance. The world, much less a person, cannot tell you what beauty is, being beautiful belongs iconically to you. Start reminding yourself that, "nothing plus no one will deter me from my PATH!" Acknowledge yourself as the most valuable individual to be loved by you! The universe is looking for your uncharted footprints across the world! Bury all your horrors one by one, the stillness of relaxing bed slumber summons you. Stop making the misstep of technology until bedtime, disconnection is irrefutable by nature. The inadequacies of irritation of self must be minimized. Your seeds of healing must be planted upon arrival of each season, remember the necessity of proper hydration. Balance your commitment to you through graduated assessments at none and established life intervals. Self-command is about asking yourself questions and supplying an educated meaningful answer in strengthening you. Overthinking happens not when you do not know, it is when you now better understand you! Unconditional love does not mean unconditional tolerance; this unlearning is vital to your mental health! Swallow what you must until you can taste what you enjoy. Dedicate you to a mediative discipline and never give up mastery of your mind, body, and spirit. Your present surroundings offer more than you receive, work on your development of soft and hard skills to deploy stronger self-esteem. Alchemize your physical prowess by self-transforming more than your physique. The eye on the prize is to maximize the stake in you. View regrets as fallen flower pedals, fertilizing minerals of foresight nutrients for forethought. An individual's particular history does not have to consecutively repeat itself; you have the power to swim to change you! Self-assessment means self-assistance equals the goal. Stop compromising what you need for wants, reposition your structure to evolve beyond having to befell you. You must morph consistently in preparing to pass the torch each time to an evolving you! Build yourself into a human of superior mental development, articulating powerful speech, and upright in stance. Your house must always champion the complete awareness of protecting you. Morally stand by overseeing yourself through kindness. Recognize then respect the collective of personalities within in you. Knowing you is within itself, knowing the Creator.

The first time you got lost, of this now discover your you!

PHILOSOPHY

Pinpoint a wending way to YOU...

Nothing and no one, shall deter me from my path...

~ Nelson ~

JOURNAL THE JOURNEY!

SELF AWARENESS

CONSISTENT ACKNOWLEDGMENT

AUTHENTIC YOU ACHIEVEMENT TRANSFORMATION

BRAND DISTRIBUTION

OWNERSHIP DIRECTION

AYA - AUTHENTIC YOU ACHIEVEMENT
Phase 2 TRANSFORMATION

What are the core values that guide your decisions and actions, and how have they evolved over time?

_____

_____

_____

_____

_____

_____

_____

_____

_____

_____

_____

_____

_____

_____

_____

_____

_____

_____

_____

_____

_____

When you face challenges, what inner strengths do you rely on most, and where do they originate from?

What brings you the deepest sense of fulfillment or peace, and why does it resonate so profoundly within you?

How do you define your purpose in life, and has that definition shifted with your experiences?

What is one belief or perspective you have held onto that you now see differently? What caused the change?

_____

_____

_____

_____

_____

_____

_____

_____

_____

_____

_____

_____

_____

_____

_____

_____

_____

_____

_____

_____

_____

How do you balance your ambitions with the need for rest and self-care? Are you doing it well?

_____

_____

_____

_____

_____

_____

_____

_____

_____

_____

_____

_____

_____

_____

_____

_____

_____

_____

_____

_____

_____

What does success look like to you beyond material or professional accomplishments?

_____

_____

_____

_____

_____

_____

_____

_____

_____

_____

_____

_____

_____

_____

_____

_____

_____

_____

What fears or insecurities do you still hold, and how do they shape your decisions or relationship with you?

_____

_____

_____

_____

_____

_____

_____

_____

_____

_____

_____

_____

_____

_____

_____

_____

_____

_____

_____

_____

_____

In moments of stillness, what thoughts or emotions rise to the surface, and what do they reveal about you?

_____
_____
_____
_____
_____
_____
_____
_____
_____
_____
_____
_____
_____
_____
_____
_____
_____
_____
_____
_____
_____

What personal sacrifices have you made for others, and how have they shaped your sense of self-knowledge?

_____

_____

_____

_____

_____

_____

_____

_____

_____

_____

_____

_____

_____

_____

_____

_____

_____

_____

_____

_____

_____

Who do you trust the most to see your authentic self, and why do you allow them that closeness?

_____

_____

_____

_____

_____

_____

_____

_____

_____

_____

_____

_____

_____

_____

_____

_____

_____

_____

_____

_____

_____

_____

When was the last time you truly felt vulnerable, and how did you handle it?

_____

_____

_____

_____

_____

_____

_____

_____

_____

_____

_____

_____

_____

_____

_____

_____

_____

_____

_____

What role does forgiveness (for yourself and others) play in your growth and peace of mind?

_____

_____

_____

_____

_____

_____

_____

_____

_____

_____

_____

_____

_____

_____

_____

_____

_____

_____

_____

How do you handle moments when your principles or integrity are tested?

_____

_____

_____

_____

_____

_____

_____

_____

_____

_____

_____

_____

_____

_____

_____

_____

_____

_____

_____

_____

_____

What past experience has left the most profound mark on your character, and how does it influence you today?

If you had to strip away all external labels (career, roles, achievements), who would you be at your core?

_____

_____

_____

_____

_____

_____

_____

_____

_____

_____

_____

_____

_____

_____

_____

_____

_____

_____

_____

_____

_____

_____

_____

_____

How do you ensure your actions align with your inner beliefs and values, even under pressure?

What does your relationship with solitude look like? Are you comfortable being alone with your thoughts?

_____

_____

_____

_____

_____

_____

_____

_____

_____

_____

_____

_____

_____

_____

_____

_____

_____

_____

_____

_____

What is one aspect of yourself that you are proud of, and how do you nurture it?

_____

_____

_____

_____

_____

_____

_____

_____

_____

_____

_____

_____

_____

_____

_____

_____

_____

_____

_____

_____

If you met your future self today, what advice or encourage-
ment would you offer?

_____

_____

_____

_____

_____

_____

_____

_____

_____

_____

_____

_____

_____

_____

_____

_____

_____

_____

_____

_____

_____

_____

What new values and principles will you establish to help shape the person you are becoming?

_____

_____

_____

_____

_____

_____

_____

_____

_____

_____

_____

_____

_____

_____

_____

_____

_____

_____

_____

_____

_____

Do you understand that you can never run out of time because you are time?

_____

_____

_____

_____

_____

_____

_____

_____

_____

_____

_____

_____

_____

_____

_____

_____

_____

_____

_____

_____

Forever love you now, though no one is watching as if you even care...

Nelson...
Sahwoo